# THE UNSAID

## FEATURING THE WINNERS OF THE GREAT INDIAN POETRY CONTEST

BY NOTION PRESS

ISBN  979-8-89699-485-5

*To all the poets brimming with
the unsaid words*

# Contents

# Reflection

*Of love, hope, dreams, the self, the world, and life itself*

# Silenced Voice

Smack, smack—do you hear that crack?
A sharp echo splitting the night's back.
It comes from Raja Bhaiya's home,
where silence holds a painful throne.

In the air hangs the weight of control,
Where peace is a price, and silence a toll.
Men once tender, now buried in shame,
under rules that strip them of their name.

"Wash the dishes," the world commands,
"Let your sister serve, you have your plans."
"Be strong, don't cry, don't show fear,
soft boys are broken, they say loud and clear."

Within him, a voice softly calls,
But it's buried beneath thick walls.
"Don't be kind," they all insist,
so he locks her in, emotions missed.

The boy grows, the scars remain,
his hands now strike to mask the pain.
The voices within him fade like rain,
hushed by a world that's always the same.

– Nanki Kandhari

# Tea – Drowning in Anger

I remember how fondly my mother used to make tea.

She would hum songs while she did,

I think back then I was still somewhat tolerable to her.

(maybe not)

She loved tea and,

She would sip on it every tragic morning and evening.

Perhaps it was her drug in a way.

But how did she end up drowning in something that she loved?

(She and I have more things in common than she thinks.)

I never drink tea.

Because whenever I see my reflection in it, all I see is my father's livid expression, her burnt face, and her gut-wrenching screams.

She still sips tea like it's nothing.

She still drinks it every tragic morning and evening.

(And I drink a glass of milk filled with guilt because she ended up saving me, but she could never save herself.)

And we never speak about what happened back then.

– Izel S.N.

# The Ache Has a Name

There's a quiet that lives in my chest,
it sounds like the creak of a door
no one ever walks through.
Like the sigh of a mirror when I stand too close,
afraid of what I might see.

I think my father taught me silence
better than he ever taught me love.
His words were knives thrown into walls,
and my mother's tears pooled in the floorboards,
where I pressed my ear and begged the wood to speak.
It never did.

At night, I dream of running,
but my feet are made of all the things I never said,
dragging, heavy, breaking open the earth beneath me.
Sometimes, I scream into my pillow,
and the sound doesn't come back.
It's swallowed by something darker than the night.

I wonder if I'll ever unlearn this ache.
If love will ever be more
than just another wound waiting to open.

– Psyche

# The Cold Embrace

The winds blew north,
the lights shining on with less force.
A crashed car below a tree,
and the ground covered with debris.

The trees stood tall,
not whimpering on a sight,
which made the crickets halt.
Many a car has passed by,
but rarely do the trees give out a sigh.

The moon's watching,
so are the tiny little birds,
eager to see if he was hurting.
Deers stopped their talk,
as they heard a sound of shock
Moments later, lights of
red and blue blink.
I realized my time began to shrink.

Men in uniform in five,
with a gurney, they arrive and try to revive.
As the last moments pass on,

I watch by as they take my body,
out of the car, into the gurney
and drive off, without knowing
I was watching.

– Alwin Baiju

# I Wish My Life Was A Prompt

I wish my life was a prompt,
so that poets could use it as a muse,
to turn it into something beautiful,
and give it some meaning and use.

I wish my life was a prompt,
so that artists could use it as a canvas,
to induce a little bit of brightness,
and give it some colour and pulse.

I wish my life was a prompt,
so that guitarists could put it to tune,
turn the madness into melody,
and immortalize it, make it a lovely boon.

I wish my life was a prompt,
so that rather than just survive,
I could absorb everything it has to offer,
and make the most of being alive.

– Satyalekha A

# The Child I Left Behind

We shatter barriers to shape emotions anew,
kneeling beneath the weight of what we never outgrew.
"Forgive me," I whisper to my heart, fractured and torn,
and to my mind, whose wisdom I've ignored and scorned.

Joy, once vibrant, fades like a forgotten song.
Memories dissolve as time drags us along.
I cry for the loss I've carried since day one,
masking my pain in facades that stun.

I've tried to outrun the past but stumble and fall,
a trembling heart knows the weight of it all.
Growth has carved me but left me undone.
Do lessons of life require breaking everyone?

"Are you okay?" I ask the child I used to be,
in a world too cold to ask the same of me.

– Prerna Madhukar

# My Cities

I remember creating cities with my hands,
with toys that thought, and lived on
with those Virtues and Vices as that of Man.

Boxes stacked atop each other,
taped, like bricks for buildings,
cemented for expensive expansions
—in futility.

I remember the toys (and myself)
becoming a catastrophe, and I being the God
to flail my arm, a thudding bolt.

They played dead charades
—horrified, frozen, torn—as I saw
with a victor on the hill of my knee,
wound up for another generation.

The next playtime would be a new age,
a new civilization, another day,
with remnants from my last time.
But I recall the Creation
and the Dismemberment of my cities

over-n-over-n-over-n-over-n-over-n-again
to know Rebirth in the eyes of That One above.

I remember playing beyond heart's content,
for such fun would be fatal
around an adult's neck.

– Hiemannk

# Self Confinement

In the quiet corners of her mind, a battle rages on.
She misses the girl to know,
Now echoes of her footsteps haunt her hope.
She has a room with no doors, no windows to see.
She's built these walls of silent decree.
Self confinement, a prison of her own,
where shadows dance, and she's alone.

In the stillness of her prison, where time seems to decay,
the window's just a memory.
A frame of light she longs to see,
yet the glass remains unbroken, a barrier to her plea.
What freedom costs, she cannot pay,
for she is both the guard and prey.
oh, to escape, to breathe, to feel.
But self made walls refuse to heal.
In this confinement, she remains the architect of her own
pain.

– Arya panda

# The Spectrum of Existence

Somewhere between the black and white lies,
a spectrum of colors—red, blue, and grey,
between hope as fresh as a blank, untouched page,
and despondency as dark as shadow's cage,
Lies the endeavor of a being.

Somewhere between veracity as pristine as white
and deceit as black as raven's flight,
Lies the gentle hues of the souls.
Between whispers of love as pure as lily,
and betrayals cloaked in pitch-dark night,
Lies a destiny that lovers must unite,
for not all things come in black or white.
Sometimes, there's a silver, hidden in sight,
a quiet glow that softens the night.

– Ambereen.vishram

# Whispers Of Confusion

I don't know what I really want to do.
Each choice I make, I'm torn in two.
I start one path, then drift from view,
Against the blue, I wander through.

My mind is clouded, full of doubt.
A swirling storm, I can't get out.
One thing I know, I can't hold true—
No single dream can grasp my hand, too.

I seek success, a shining light.
But with this heart, I fear the fight.
For with this restlessness in me,
I wonder if success will ever be.

– Nidhi Bhargava

# Isn't It Beautiful?

Isn't it beautiful?
How hands fit perfectly into each other
like two molds of clay,
no cracks in its shape.
How butterflies land on fresh green leaves.
A camera will never capture the beauty our eyes can see.

Isn't it rare?
How two people come together,
a bond is formed,
they cherish it forever.
How the strings of invisibility exist all around, tying us
to one another,
somehow we are found.

Isn't it sweet?
How words can heal,
how we all find happiness in giggles and wet streets.
We jump into puddles and dance in the rain, nothing
else can take away the pain.

Isn't it beautiful?
How the world is,
you lose sight of it so easily,
but it still exists.

– parenthesis

# Suddenly I Know

My eyes race to the door before you can even enter through.
The soft thud of your steps, hand on the knob, I can almost see through the door and I see you.
Maybe loving you gives me superpowers that I myself cannot fathom, because I'd know your presence anywhere.
I'd know it without looking up because for me you're always there and when you walk in, there's nothing else.

You've made me write, you've made me rhyme.
You've made me dream, make up stories in my mind.
Before I even knew it, I put down my guard,
placed airpods in my ear, listening to the language of my heart.

Like an array of dominoes, I watched scenes fly,
watched your secret smile, found myself looking into your eyes.
All I've ever wanted is all you've ever wanted too.
And suddenly I know the guy of my dreams is you.

– Jiya Doshi

# Lovely Manipulation

Stressed with ocean-deep regrets,

lies that fly sky high,

a wrinkle-free face when you're disappointed.

You could make a murder look just fine.

Never saw such a fine trickster,

someone who can easily articulate.

Even your beauty manipulates.

Your hollow claims of not being a 'narcissist', but have you heard your voice, which always says, "C'mon, let's talk about me!"

You were born to do this.

To be an unforgettable lesson for a naive human.

Guess you're not totally wrong when you showed me the keys to the cage for the last time; I accept my mistake of not running away.

Only till it empties the hourglass, I need time to make high walls that no storm can now trespass.

I have learned it all, I swear, no space for even a single tear.

– Ayushi

# The Mess

The battle of my mind
wouldn't stop any time.
I look so calm and fine,
but my head's a mess every night.
The echoes of your screaming,
I am still day dreaming.
Should I scream or should I cry?
'Cause things aren't anywhere near fine.
I imagine and create
the bubble of reality that you break.
Why tell me it's all a lie?
Don't you like being on cloud nine?
Said so many words,
now I can't deny.
My mind is a mess.
And no one knows why.

– Kajal Singh

# Grey

Am I the beaming light of the sun or the darkness of night?
Tormented by a war that I can no longer fight.

Or am I a letter stuck in an envelope waiting for
someone to open?
Not to romanticise but to slowly unfold and read me
like no one.

Am I the colour grey
that has confusion running in its DNA,
and a dolorous Duality that screams?
Or am I a window, which acts as a bridge to the inside
and outside world but it itself rots in between?

Maybe I am waiting to be a rainbow until the very end
of the storm.
Or maybe I am just a flicker or a dust of a star that is
not yet born.

– Sanika pawar

# Unfiltered Me

Look at my scars. Pretty, ehw na? But it's alright. I embrace them as they are. I wear them with quiet pride.

Wanna see my insecurities?

Small, underweight, a tiny creature am I. A bit introverted, a bit shy. Yeah, I often need no reasons to cry.

Acne and dark circles, paints a picture of restless nights, silent battles fought in the dead of night.
A complexion too kissed by the sun. Standing small, behind glasses that shape my view.

Mental breakdowns, silent screams in my mind.
Moments when the world feels too heavy,
and hope is hard to find.
Yet, here I stand, a mosaic of imperfections,
This is me, unfiltered. And that's how I am designed.

– Oshii

# Mirror!

The demons in my head are consuming me.
Day by day their cussing voices are getting louder .
A little child in my heart is screaming out of despair.
But someone is choking my throat,
so that her screams will never get heard.
She's trying to break all the restraints,
but the hold in my throat is too firm.
I can feel its tightness all around my neck.
As, in pain, I stood in front of the Mirror,
now I see crystal clear,
The Demons,
The li'l child,
And the person who is choking me;
They all are there,
in the — Mirror.

– Pavi

# What If I Die Someday?

What if I die someday?
Will you look for me?
Up in the sky,
where the stars twinkle, the moon shines,
Or maybe in the garden,
Where florets blossom, trees gently sway.

What if I die someday?
Will you look for me?
Between the pages of books,
where each word narrates our longing tale.
Or maybe in the sea,
where each wave is full of memories.

What if I die someday?
Will you look for me?
Beneath the warmth of the sunlight,
or in the melody of our favourite song,
where each lyric is a flashback into our past.

– Ishita Tiwari

# Between The Lips

I hold the brown leaves between my lips,
the way a womanizer holds those hips.
Every smoke I take in becomes my breath,
and like a scar, it marks a stain on my teeth.
Somewhere between the fire and the ashes,
I found myself numb, like frozen eyelashes.

While I held onto this invisible grip,
like a ringmaster of the circus without a whip,
I could feel humanity's death wish,
growing inside, like the smell of rotten fish.
I could feel it crawling beneath my skin—
The love for destruction, war, and the need behind
every sin.
With this burden, I took a cigarette and lit,
to relive it all again—the fire, the smoke, and every bit.

– Midhun Thotathil

# Empty Solitude

I reached out,
hoping for a touch of your warmth,
a sliver of your attention.
But all I found was coldness,
a chasm I couldn't cross.

Your indifference was a dagger,
your absence, a wound that never heals.
I wanted nothing more
than to be seen,
to be loved by you.

But in the silence,
In the space where you should have been,
I realized the bitter truth:
I was never truly meant to be yours.

So I learned to find strength within,
to mend the cracks and heal the scars.
I built myself anew,
without the shadow of your love,
emerging whole, despite the void you left.

– Paridhi

# The Heart of Home

Home is in
> Warmth
>> Love
>>> Happiness
>>>> Nostalgia

When I wear my mother's clothes,
it feels like a soft hug from her—
a hug that would not let the world hurt me.
It feels like her soft hands,
which would pet my head the whole night to make me
fall asleep.

Love is when anywhere in the world feels like home
with him by my side.
Even in the coldest place,
I feel the warmth
when we hold hands.

When my father walks in,
the house lights up with a spark of bliss.
The air fills with joy and happiness,
as the long-awaited holiday

reunites the family after so long.
The home feels like HOME.

Being around this group of friends,
I return to my teenage self.
Memories come back to us
with laughter and nostalgia,
like a hug from our past selves.

– Sadaf Ansari

# An Artist's Fragmented Soul

The sculptures I carved behind the curtains,
each piece a trace of her, molded by my trembling hands.
The songs I sang on empty stages were hers alone,
for we loved each other in secrecy, behind closed doors.
We danced in silence, we kissed in shadows,
a love so alive, it left scars that held its truth long after it
faded.

You say I have crossed a line?
That my hands, trembling with devotion,
carved madness where they sought only meaning?
The river I painted in the desert of my loneliness,
was it nothing but an illusion?
A mirage born from the thirst of my soul,
fading the moment I reached for it?

So let it be.
If my solace is an illusion, let me sleep undisturbed.
For in the asylum of my mind,
I held her once, and that was enough.

– Shreya

# Neem's Whisper

Under the neem tree, I lie so still,
the wind's soft whisper, a soothing thrill.
Does the old tree weep, or is it just the hill?
Sleep's gentle arms, my senses fill.

"I have seen it all," said the old tree,
"Your grandpa's life, wild and free.
He worked the fields, with heart and hand,
A farmer true, across the land.

"I have seen him sow and reap,
watched his children laugh and weep.
His love for cattle, never in vain.
He stood strong and steady, through the sun and rain.

"Though years went by, his spirit bright,
he wandered freely, morning to night.
His hair turned silver, but hope still grew,
like tender plants bathed in morning dew.

"His body's gone, but his soul still stays,
Like a whisper on warm, sunny days."

Tears rolled down my eyes, I felt his grace,
His love lives on in this sacred place.

– Sindhu Selvi

# Paradox

Mom, I hate you—
Not in the way you think.
I hate you for loving me
when I'm not deserving of it,
For seeing the good in me
when all I see is darkness,
For holding on to hope
when I've lost all mine,
For being my lifeline
when I'm drowning in my mind.

Your love is a weight
that presses down on me,
A constant reminder
of all my failures and flaws.
A burden I can't bear.
A debt I can't repay.
A love that's suffocating.
A love that's killing me.
But still, you love me.
Through all my anger and pain,
Through all my hate and shame,

You love me, Mom. You love me.
And I hate you for it—
For loving me unconditionally,
For loving me when I can't love myself.

– Tarun Kanumane

# The Weight of Waiting

Tired of waiting,
I gaze in the mirror's face.
A lost dreamer stares back,
a failure in this place.

Hopelessness creeps in,
like a thief in the night.
Stealing joy,
leaving only tears and endless fight.

Unworthy of happiness—
That's what I've been told.
Hard to love,
a heart that's grown cold.

My waiting will be constant,
a never-ending plight.
Alone, lost in loneliness,
longing for a glimmer of light.

God's least favorite child—
That's how I feel.
Forgotten and forsaken,
my soul begins to reveal.

The pain of waiting,
the ache of being alone.
A lost dreamer,
longing for a love that's never known.

My heart is a heavy burden,
weighed down by the wait.
A soul that's lost its purpose,
a life that's lost its fate.

The darkness closes in,
a suffocating embrace.
A life without love,
a soul forever lost in this space.

– Neha Karmakar (Shayarisha)

# How Was I To Know?

How selfish am I?
Can see the pain and not the cause,
Just want to weep all your tears,
Still your greatest grief in front of me,
Holding this piece of cloth for you,
Looking at you, how dreadful you look,
But unaware of the truth.

Years pass on.
Look at you, nothing changed.
You want me to get changed.
Your telephone ringing in my ears,
And look, I cut off the cables.

How guilty am I?
I made you like that, maybe half-dead.
This horrific spectacle in front of me,
You weep and this time it's anger.
I'm holding my mistakes, giving you more of it,
But still unaware of the truth.

Years pass on.
We used to be best friends,
And now I became your worst enemy.
But still long to know you more,
As you are my everything.

– Avni S.

# Shelter

When four walls make one shelter,
there is no window to surface things
under the shadow, far from the light,
where every act becomes a burden
for all the members to quietly witness,
being cemented in stillness,
inherently robbed of any expression.

Whether love or animosity, fear or squabble,
each page turns in front of the naked eye,
the dwelling mind, the running heart,
as one naive corner observes hostility,
between the two pillars of strength,
who support and hold the house together,
tremble with disputes and agitation.

The changing seasons play their part,
with cracks widening all over the place.
They are treated haphazardly, at times,
by covering them with new paint.

Unfortunately, the inner rust keeps rising,
until the house finally falls, unable to bear
the pressure of a broken establishment,
numbing and shedding every corner away.

– Raj Darji

# The Lost Essence

Something I thought was mine, flew away from me.

An essence I possessed without knowing it was never mine.

A shadow I kept in innocence, held onto in quiet unknowing.

You were like the rain I failed to relish in and the dream I couldn't forever live in, for I was destined to be the color but never your painting.

Just like that you vanished into the past yet to be waned into oblivion.

As you bloomed bright, my petals fell, lingering in the thought of why.

And just like that, I walked away, wanting to turn back but knowing I was the thread you never wanted to grasp.

– Emy Elizebath Oommen

# Dreamers

She gazes in awe,
as the clouds cradle her dreams,
the breeze brushes her cheeks—
warm, like her lover's graze.

The thin, knowing fingers,
tracing the known path,
lingers too long.
Clouds blush in the reverence,
witnessing the voyage of rebellion.

A voyeur to her quiet surrender,
the once-tender breeze,
teasing with shameless intent.
Each caress unapologetic,
unrestrained...

The clouds smirk at her quiet submission,
billowing with whispered laughter,.
Her hair dances with the giddy wind,
each strand spilling a hushed secret.

The space drips in silence,
in the mirage of illusion,
drunk in the lovers oblivion,
spilling the poison
of unfortunate union,
of two diabolic dreams.

Dreamers, lost in clouds,
sucked by earth,
lost its essence,
moulded into one.

Air hushes their voice,
breeze hides their bare flesh,
clouds snicker at their giddiness,
And the Earth, ever watchful,
laughs in joy.

– Sudrisha Chakraborty

# In Thy Eyes

How fickle is fate's hand upon thee,
yet, even in union, a distant plea.
Behold, thy eyes and words, they tell,
how thy form wilted, thy essence fell.
Through silent queries, a heart's dance,
beyond the lips, dreams take their chance.

In thy hands, the lines unfold,
narratives untold, stories bold.
Why eludes sorrow's grasp thy tongue?
Unveil the ache where melodies are sung.

My heart bears witness to thy plight.
What I fail to speak, takes flight.
Tell me, what shall I do
for thee to see my heart's story too?
Call to me, I'll weather all rue.
Speak once more, and once more, anew!

No longer shall we part ways.
Here we'll stay, come what may.
This is love's saga, steadfast and strong,
destined to endure lifelong.

– Madiha Naaz

# A Prisoner's Lament

I walked out free, or so it seemed.
Iron gates behind, but chains unseen.
Each step I took, the weight grew worse.
Home a dream, now a cruel curse.

They stole my years, my innocence died,
buried deep, where truth can't hide.
Memories haunted, nights I fought
for faces I loved, for a life forgot.

But the world had turned, it shut me out.
Eyes once warm now brimmed with doubt.
The hugs were gone, replaced by frost.
In silence, they spoke: "You're already lost."

A stranger here, where I yearned to stay.
Time had stripped their love away.
My scars repaid with scorn and lies,
their hearts moved on, their pity dry.

Free in flesh, but damned in soul,
a relic left to rot alone.
This life I craved now takes its toll—
The real prison is this hollow home.

– Mightypen

# The Crowd's Agony

The sun doesn't set anymore.
I sit atop a boulder and listen to roses wail in the heavy
wind.
They scream and cry and I listen to their pain.
If I nipped them off, would I be considered insane?

They cry and they cry and they cry.
The boulder is warm under the sun.
The thorns prick me for attention.
I close my eyes and they call me selfish.

The roses whisper among themselves.
The trees sway in anger and protest.
"My legs are tied. I can't walk," I scream.
The chaos continues as my voice drowns out.

I drown one rose and deprive another.
The ropes on my legs rub against my skin.
I walk and I walk and I walk.
Until they are far away enough,

But I hear them in my head now.
"Selfish, selfish soul," they're saying.
And I nod as I fall to my knees.

– Sansita Pradeep

# Pearl Drops

She walks with a heart too heavy,
full of emotions rippling like waves,
cresting, breaking, pulling her under.
She blames herself for feeling too much,
for the storms inside her chest.
But isn't that her beauty?
Isn't that what makes her, 'HER'?

Every tear that escapes her lashes
is a pearl,
a piece of her soul
crystallized in sorrow,
evidence of her depth.

When the world strips her bare,
when the weight is too much,
she holds her sadness within.
Her tears pause at the edge of her eyes,
forming a fragile dam,
turning them into oysters,
guarding treasures only she can hold.

But even oysters crack.
When her tears finally fall,
they don't just carry pain;
they carry her story—
a quiet scream,
a girl who felt too much
and gave everything,
even when empty.

– Priyanka Sani

# The Last Dream

I burned my soul to light their way,
gave all my nights to build their day.
Each step I took was not for me,
but for a dream they'd one day see.

I fought the storms, I bore the pain,
hid my tears in the pouring rain.
Built them wings while mine were torn,
a blazing star, now forlorn.

I dreamed of heights, a boundless sky,
a passionate kid who dared to fly.
But dreams die slow in a loveless fight,
and now I dwell in eternal night.

No hand reached out, no "Why?" was heard,
just empty echoes of unspoken words.
The hell I built to keep them free
became the chains that imprisoned me.

So here I lie, my spirit dry.
The last dream fades as I ask, "Why?"

– Jayu

# Yearning

Your absence is a silence I've grown acclimated to.
I moved on.
I laugh hard at the jokes you used to listen to.
Looking ahead, leaving my doubts gone.
I still go to our favorite place for the chicken you used to rave about.
I aced that interview we talked about.
I still go around using your favorite phrases.
I-do-not-miss-you.
I'm just fond of your favorite places.
Or do I miss you?
Your absence echoes.
Your shadows linger.
In every bite of the chicken I savor.
In every technique in my interview.
Even in death, you remain an uninvited persistent guest.

BUT

Without you, the world's rhythm feels off key.
One less person to inspire change.
A hand less to lend.
One less positivity to spread.
And even in death,

you live on.
In the lives you have touched.
In the radiance you emit-ed.
Even in death, you are alive.


– Rodiyah

# What's Mine?

A thought weighs heavy, sharp as a knife—
Is anything mine in this fleeting life?
The face I see, a blur in the glass,
sometimes whole, sometimes broken, alas.
Is it mine?

If it is, why does it feel so empty?
This heartbeat, these breaths, do they belong to me?
The days that slip by, the nights that consume,
the sky above, this suffocating room.
Are they mine?

The tears that fall, are they my own?
Or are they echoes of the pain I've known?
If they are mine, why do they seem so far?
If they are mine, why can't I heal the scar?

Even my breath, it feels foreign, strange,
As if life itself is slipping from range.
Is anything truly mine, or am I lost in time?
Am I even mine, or just a hollow rhyme?

– Himanshu Ansh

# Good Girl

Every time she did something that pleased him,
he called her a "good girl"
and put a feather to her cap.
Now, she's got so many of those feathers
that she's turned into a peacock.
She started tap dancing everytime
he played a game of 'Simon says rain'.
She twirled and swayed to his tune,
flicking off her tears as rain.
She flashed a siren of blue...green...blue...green...,
hoping that someone would listen to her.
But everyone was deaf to the
haunting music that only she heard.
It was only the ocean who responded and
blinked back blue...green...blue...green...
Was it any wonder that one day
her body was found ashore the sand.
His red flag had smothered
all the green goodness in her and
now her body only flashed blue.

Blue nails.
Blue lips.
Blue body.

– Meenu Maria Jose

# The Woods

The woods speak to me,
of pedlars and their trekking boots crunching on dry
leaves,
and the blossoming flowers
sucked on by the buzzing bees.

The woods speak to me,
as I trace their valiant scars
of the cold nights
spent under a sky full of stars,
While the burning beast fed
on its helpless hunted prey,
and the rain showered down
on where the empty carcass lay.

The woods speak to me
of all the wonders they have seen,
like the snow covered forest floor
that turns to white from green,
the frolics of the babies
while their mothers walk in herds,
and the unified symphony
of the chirpy little birds.

The woods speak to me
in a language of their own,
of aromas and touches
and light breezes blown.
The woods have entered me
and entwined with my soul.
I wait earnestly every day
aAs new tales unfold.

– Debayani Sengupta

# Dilemma of Knowing

Has the world gone mad or have I become sane?
What is not yet felt? When did it last rain?
What is known of love and what is known of hate?
And how can it be trusted, if life hasn't yet met with fate?
To know what has sunk deep, the skin must've drowned
a feel somewhere shallow,
If the beam that was seen was infinite, the eyes must've
met before with a finite glow.

– Janvi

# Dreams With You

When you're surrounded by the cold,

try to find the things that warm you anyway.

The weather, a cup of coffee, cozy-warm arms around you,

the bookshelf with the ladder to go up as you need more coffee to wake.

Annotation books, memories, bookmarks, hand-written letters

the future in which we live more collectively.

Vegetable garden and a

tiny cookie store with a hanging bell at the entrance.

Large library with couches and vintage lamps,

conversation with your favourite person about books,

comfy pajamas for a comfy bed.

The train ticket for Platform 9 ¾

the road trip to Banaras,

with every place, you've been marked in RED!

– Bobby

# The Swathe Mirror

As I look into the void of life,
all I can see is a man who despises.
A man who despises his life.
A man who can't look himself in the eyes.
The more he looks, the more he thinks,
every second with every blink
He stares at the pitch black mirror which gives him a past filled with glimmers.
Disappointment is what he gets with every look he gives.
At last he figures that it is the mirror of life which is pitch black yet so bright.
A mirror that tells the crux of life.

– Rudransh Paroha

# sepia

Sepia moon and the sepia stars,
that span across the black black sky.
May you not hide beneath,
the yellow stare of the streetlight?

The wind, cold again, brings the fog in
to dine with me, and they cross
the little window I've left open
in my little whitewashed room.

Switch off the lights to see you,
the Moon, who you so gloriously
let the moonshine fall into my pillow,
and pet my washed hair and brush it off.

Memories that you have, always had,
since then until now, and long forgotten after—
isn't life just a curated pickle, at best, at last,
served best at nights with comfort food?

Watering mouths will become teary eyes,
but then how could I not see your little,
little, little craters of moondust,
that gathers around like oil in a pickle?

– Udbhas Kumar Bhoi

# Silent Nights

In the loudest city
where sirens howled,
a man lay still,
under the night's shroud.

In his trembling hand,
a crumbled picture
of a boy whose joy
now is a whisper.

His mind wandered
streets, astray,
through narrow lanes
where dreams escape,
and crowded paths
where shadows play,
in search of his son,
a familiar face.

Drenched in sorrow,
anguish, and pain,
he longed for peace
within heaven's reign.

Roars and whimpers
within his mind,
chaos so crippling,
he cried and cried.

He hoped,
for one more night,
among the wails
and broken lights,
to hear his son
laugh with delight,
safe in his arms
where everything felt right.

– Kushi Jathanna

# A Lover's Secret

They wait annoyed in the traffic,
hoping for it to move fast.
But my heart wants it to stop still,
to stay stuck forever

As I admire the star of my heart,
dozing off on the passenger's seat,
the star that made my heart bloom
without her knowing.

She looks so precious,
as she softly mumbles
in the daze of a dream.
Hopefully, it's about me.

Enchanted I am
by the blush creeping on her cheeks
by her not-so-subtle snores
and her hair strands all messy.

But a harsh honk shakes me,
forces me to rev up the engine,
while all I want to do
is to keep smiling foolishly.

Reaching her abode,
I call her name so gently,
and she opens her eyes slightly,
mumbling something incoherent.

Grabs her purse slowly,
and with a goodbye, exits the car,
leaving me all alone
with a little secret of my own.

– Neilaanjana Srivastava

# The Longing Void

"I need my space", I used to keep complaining
when she used to takeover the entire bed,
leaving me a tiny little corner to curl.

The bed feels more spacious now,
but it's a cruel illusion.
It's a longing void she has left behind,
one that my heart can never ignore.

I still sleep on my side,
my body stubbornly clinging onto the habit,
refusing to invade the space that was once hers.

In the darkness of the cold night,
I pull my blanket over me.
I miss the tug of war we played every night for the blanket.
I miss the warmth that SHE gave me.

Your gentle snores...like a chirping bird
are replaced by an eerie silence.

The safe haven of your cuddles lost,
my body shivers in fear of loneliness.

The longing void remains,
in the bed and in my heart.

– G2

# The Hate Poem

I don't know if I want to forget you.
Deep in between the starry nights I stay awake,
your faded memories dancing in me like the ripples over
a lake.
Low as the tide that hits
is what I feel about the fact that we might never meet.
I miss having those warm eyes over mine,
those pretty smiles you had everyday,
the way you walked, the way you talked.

Everything about you is like the profound art
that sometimes made me feel the lack of breath.
But, my love, all I have in my little heart.
Without you, my life is simply a heathe.

I promise I'm not trying to be clichè.
It ties and twists and stings my soul how much you hate me.
I swear I hate you too.
But again I stay awake thinking.
Do I love you much more than I can take?

– Liya

# Uncomfortable Conversations, Sitting Through The Evenings

We are small, altered beings.
We are not wise, and not very often kind.
We don't sit with our grief, nor of others.
On most days, we prefer to drink that tea alone.
Unknowingly, we move from one thought to another.
We keep moving in the little spaces of our mind.

Someone once told me.
We confront our fears in our dreams.
But I am convinced I confront it better in my poems.

It has always been difficult for me to leave,
for me to return after I leave.
When Plath writes, "Is there no way out of the mind?"
I look at the words, sincerely, I hope.
I would like to be there, outside and free. Listen,

I think I have been waiting for a poem for too long,
I should leave.

– Radhika Darshetkar (noor)

# And The Clock Strikes Midnight

To whom do I owe the greatest apology?
To the person I became or the one I couldn't?
To the one who got killed?
Or the one that didn't?
And what if they cross paths?
Different lifelines but the same darn clock.
False god to false applauses,
one chased the spotlight,
the other gave her all
but never really got it right.
Yet, they feel so alive, for the first time,
with no one to watch.
For they cried themselves to sleep,
preaching "nobody gets me".
Yet, it felt so right.
So why did they end themselves this time?
They look through the creeks of their childhood home,
and it's best believed that no one is home.
They turned out to be the most fulfilled
when stranded all alone.

– Arpita Singh

# Life: The Push and The Pull

Isn't it strange that each day, each moment in life's grand tone,

we are expected to breathe, speak, meet, bond, and then disown?

Find new people, work, dreams, and keep seeking the new,

while letting go of breaths, bonds, people, and dreams we once knew.

We are told, "Life keeps moving, so you move on too."

Even though we want to hold on, to "PULL" those in our milieu.

Yet, life, like a river, moves on, "PUSHES" us to flow, forcing us to grow, though the process is slow.

The chaos triggers change, guiding us to find our own way.

No matter how close and dear, we must part someday.

It's a strange disturbing dynamic, this cycle of "PUSH" and "PULL,"

where moving on makes space for the new, making life full.

– Maitry Shah

# A Love Letter to Love

Dear Love,
my childhood playmate,

If we meet again in this lifetime,
can we please go back to splashing in puddles on rainy days?
How about preserving the last autumn leaf like memories inside our slam books?
or,
What if we pretend to be ancient explorers creeping through the labyrinths of the decaying castle of hope?

and maybe promise...

to frolic down the meandering lanes of life,
to reach our graves,
        hand in hand,
    wrinkled but firm,
    celebrating eternity in transience.

– Sayatri

# Late Afternoon

Your shadow longer than silence,
we're two brackets of almost —
suspended between here and somewhere else.

I saw your story in the way
you adjusted your backpack:
half-packed dreams, half-forgotten plans.

Who knows how many lives
brush past each other
in these breathing spaces
where nothing and everything
happen at once?

– UJJAWAL DAWNA

# Red

I have always wondered about the way I'll lose my life.
Will it be an accident?
Will my car crash?
Will I become an unknown victim of a  homicidal maniac?

But turns out,
it was the thread of your love that hanged my fate,
and I tightened the noose every time you looked away.
You stopped writing me letters so I replaced the ink with my blood.
If it wasn't my life at least
my death can bring you to my door.

You can kill me with a machete or
strangle me with your hands.
Take the matchsticks from the fifth drawer to send me straight to hell.
Just don't lunge for my heart
before you slit my wrists.
Let my last breath capture the way

your brown eyes sparkle in sunset.
The way they love the colour red.
- justawallflower


– Payal Taparia

# Litost

Me and Mama on an evening.
A small screen, a fairytale in it.
Or not.
As her hand, bigger than mine,
fell upon my eyes,
I hear the slash of a sharp.
'The wind?',
my little mind thought.

Me and Mom on an afternoon.
A small black screen after a girl who bleeds.
Her villain in this movie is 'she'.
The blade kissed her wrist.
Neither regret nor guilt did she commit.
'Why hurt herself?' my thin voice to my mother.

Me and my mother at night.
A small flashing screen with headlines.
A weed plucked.
And the mother couldn't believe it.
As her dove, dove a little too deep
in an ocean full of grey no one swims in.

My mother on a morning.
A small black screen with no reflection.
As the flame flickered.
As she wept.
The small black screen
me and my mother watched after dawn.

– nameless

# If Death Finds Me

If death finds me,
may it find me alive
in the stories untold & the words I left behind.
If tomorrow starts without me,
may my soul finally set free.

If death finds me,
may it find me alone,
with only shadows,
where love was once called home
& in the darkness.
May I find peace.
A sorrowful end to a life ceased.

If tomorrow starts without me,
may the words I left behind
become my legacy,
connecting my soul to minds

May they whisper my name.
In the silence, may they hear my voice

to know that I lived, that I loved in vain.
May my legacy be a lasting sigh
in the stories I told & the words I left behind.

– KB♥

# Hades visits me on pasta nights

Hades comes to visit me on the nights I make pasta, and we sit on the floor and talk about life as if it was a lost lover.

Scars all over his body, he wants to grab someone's hand and run in the streets but he is afraid.

Of everything: the way he fell down once and scraped his knees,

the way Acheron run in his veins,

and the way it reminded him of all the children who got hurt.

The way he is afraid to bleed it away so he puts a bandage with a flower on it.

Hades blushes every time he talks about flowers.

He shows me the pomegranate seeds he carries around,

to plant on the places every flower died.

He says how grief is the only way he knows love and death is the only way he knows life.

So, we close our eyes, hold our hands and pretend we are running, somewhere really far.

– Rayne Addams

# Resistance

*Against norms, chains, injustice, and silence*

# "White looks good on you"

you said with a beguiling smile,
and now I am done wearing white.

When did my favourite colour
become imprints of invisible debauchery,
a tear in the fabric of my propriety?
Every night, my brain plays
the montage of our secret
rendezvous (on loop)—
noxious fluid swells up to my chest
as your cartographer's fingers draw
miles and miles of lines
over the curves of my body,
leaving trails in the sultry sweat
over and over and over
till my flesh quicksands
and bones crack.

You didn't hear when I said, ""Stop"".
You just cared about the meat
wrapped inside saran wrap,
even when it turned cold.

I don't know how to stop this feeling
or, more precisely, how to kill it.

How many days do I have to pretend to stand still
before someone notices the roots of
the scarred night's memory
spreading, strangling, and encroaching
beyond my control?

– Boranya Choudhury

# A Letter to the Child Within Us

It's strange how we grow,
hearing of trust, love, and respect.
Yet, no one ever taught us
how to feel them,
or what to do when they break.

As children, we simply trusted,
loved without question,
believed without fear.
But somewhere along the way,
we lost the map to that magic.

Now we say, "You broke my trust."
But haven't we broken our own?
The quiet faith of the child inside,
the one who dreamed
and dared to hope.

That child still watches—
Would they smile at the life we've made?
Or weep at the weight we carry?

Maybe it's time to forgive ourselves,
to mend what's been undone,
and remember how to believe again.

– Sanely_sam

# Enquiries

In the shadows we lie low,
not of want or will.
The light offers itself,
only to those deemed fit.
The law of the land,
where the great cast labels.
To rise up against, very few are able.
Humans born of the same kind and species,
yet different in the way of treatment.
Trembling historians
flip through pages red.
Thundering politicians—
Speeches that never seem to end.
What for is this naive consciousness?
To remove the shackles of discrimination?
Or to free one and find the next victim?
Of birth our fates are prewritten,
not by the stars,
but by corrupt vile minds.

Yet we live in a land of the "free"?
Who understands the caged bird of the mind?
Who determines who holds the key?

– Grayirin

# More Than a Chatter

I know you're tired of hearing about rape.

So are we.

Strolling down the alley where the moon stands high.

Shadows lurking in sight of glowing skin.

"Speak up" they said, when the words get loud, blind is the crowd.

Blame it on the booze and enticing flesh.

The wound etched in the deep, forgets to trust the saint.

At times, the crook is a wanderer.

In fleeting verse, it's a dearer. But it's not all men, for sure.

Still, the watcher watches, like a distant blaze,

and point fingers, blaming ashes.

Born with fear, a disgraced verity of daises alike.

The fire is the crime, the ashes the victims,

but the fault, they place on the latter.

A twisted truth, a broken system.

An issue that needs more than just a chatter.

– Lakshmy S

# Rubies and Pearls

"Rouge, ma belle",
The visitors in white whine.
Chased the clouds to stain it red.
Darling little bub, loveliest of them all,
went oblivion to its dripping scarlet.
They hid their tintless linens.
They latched their spined doors.
They perfumed their pure satins.
They sheltered their white roses.

What rule book of wrong doing was it,
to delight in pearls when stitched in rubies?
A moonshine offered a piece of fair string,
and she crafts a pendant out of it.
Other lights of goodwill waited all over.
The dark road, gifting more fair thread.
And she stood in their graciousness,
weaving the roots of her world
in the serenity of glorious white,
turning white into her legacy.

– Serene Puja

# Clothes on the Line

The clothes are drying on the line,
as they have been for days.
Their roof is slowly falling off,
a house's rent, they can't pay.

Little children play barefoot,
poking fun at farm cattle nearby.
And the stoic creatures stand
without water, barely alive.

Hunger strikes the stomach,
but the women busy themselves.
Dare not think of pots and pans,
or they'll cry over empty shelves.

Dark clouds now shower rain,
the clothes on the line, sodden,
but no one even seems to care,
dancing in their barren gardens.

– Tejasvi R A

# An Odd Sheep

A soft side writes crime.
Incomplete is a poetry of mine,
Limits are what is preached.
Empty has my soul reached.

One view of freedom I dream,
crushed by the worldly scream
I turn around and see a child,
mount of curses on the new soul piled.

Beneath my cold skin, fiery rage is boiling.
There is another Art, I see they are spoiling.
"This is not done in a sophisticated way,
Her words and arts are abnormal," they say.

All she did was to paint the truth
and society calls her an absurd youth.
She abandoned painting and poetry.
To be "right" in their way, she lives in misery.

The more she listens,
more she burns.
The more she lives,
more she yearns.

At a blank page her soul sunk deep,
her conscience shattering piece by piece.
She drinks coffee to sleep,
poisoned it to live in peace.

– Hardee Vora

# Daily Bread

She was petite.
They kept on asking,
"Don't you eat?"
She replied,
"No, I devour."

I devour unsolicited opinions.
It has thorns,
it hurts but I devour.
I devour the contempt,
of not being conventionally pretty,
It has spikes,
it pains but I devour.

I devour the denigration,
of being skinny
It has specules,
it strains but I devour.
Yes, I eat a lot,
of the debris, the dross.

I eat it all,
odds and ends, slags and all,

born out of the distorted beauty standards,
residing rent free everywhere,
thrown upon me every time,
sucking the joy
ruthlessly.
I devour all of it.
But 'weight' a constant,
nonchalant, callous.

She replied back,
the opinions unasked,
don't they work?
I receive them as piecemeals,
ready to consume,
some as granules, some as morsels.
I receive them in large packets,
ready to gobble,
I devour, devour them all,
yet, futile it remains.
It's hefty,
Yet weight, a constant!
An unresolved puzzle.
"No, I don't starve.
I devour."

– Amrutha.S

# The Sceptic's Admonition

Dystopia plays hide n' seek,
the soldiers march and cry,
the King struts to utopia,
while the poets choke and die.

Close your eyes and draw the blinds,
the boy is crying wolf again.
"Beware! a sycophant in sheep's clothing,
is more treacherous than a villain!"

Will you use your last life?
or are you scared of strife?
Click on resume before
your screen, game over, lights.

How long will you go on
in your contagious blithe,
in this passive existence,
while the King, unchecked, reigns?

The lute, webs of twisted truth spins,
the lyre screams and breaks its strings,

John's mice will die in Hamelin,
while the pied piper, lullaby, sings.

"mirror, mirror" head for the hills,
before "off with your head" the Queen trills!

– Anushka Choudhary

# Prodigy

You can bring her or him,
poor or rich, wise or dumb.
You can read and write,
or even against time,
show will or might,
maybe even let your passion kill.

But

In their eyes, you will always be a doctor or engineer.
Even if your hands shake from stethoscopes,
or your mind races reading C++,
you will always be the same.

You and Sharma ji ka beta,
or the topper girl in your colony,
maybe the child prodigy with dark circles,
or the underdog with one dream.

But you will never be an artist, never a poet, never a
photographer.
And never the art, never the poem and never the photo.

To them, you will always be a doctor and engineer, and never the patient, nor the project.

– Avika Das

# A Woman's Place

An age-old tale, this is not,
but ancient roots this sure has got.

Seeds of sexism grew in the wild,
fuelled by entitlement that patriarchy piled.

Untamed and raw into vicious parasites they
pullulate,
living off a society authored by men to dictate.

What was left behind was a society ignorant to
this spread,
as they made the decision to go for the easy and
inherit it instead.

"Genesis 2:22- And the rib which Lord has taken
from man
made he a woman and brought her unto the
man".

Debt of a rib turned into a rent.
Rent for a place that for her too was meant.

What a strange curse that has dawned upon,
as we still pay a rent for a place that has been
long gone.

– Anagha

# Promise to My Motherland

Years have passed
since I left your soil.
In pursuit of dreams,
I set foot on a foreign land to toil.

I speak proudly to the world
of your achievements and successes
through my journey,
which has led me to many addresses.

Forces diverse may have tainted your patience,
as shades of grief have ravaged our nation.
The youth you have nourished have risen
and will rise magnificently to restore your ascension.

You gave me the wings to fly
and explore realms far and wide.
But like a child to a mother
I will return one day to your side.

With noble deeds small and grand,
to amplify the glories of our tricolor,
to paint our country's future with hues of
success, prosperity and valor.

With ideas shrewd and bold,
sparkling with hopes of reform,
I will return to serve my part,
come hail or thunder or storm.

– Nirupa Raghavan

# Your Daughter

I asked the god,
"Why did you give me life through my mama?"
I have tried to go away but the longing for her just gets
me back to her.
She reaches out to me just to make me suffer.
While I ask her,
"Do you really want me to live a life like yours?
Will you be pleased if I suffer the same and have the
same tears?
Just accept me as a kid, not your healer."

I am also a kid just like my brother.
Maybe grab me in your arms,
sharing your warmth,
like you do for him when he needs it.
Let me cry just like a child,
maybe just accept me as yours.
Just move your fingers above my head,
like you did to brother when he was sad.
Or maybe just give me a hot tea
just as you gave it to father.

– Palak giri

# Mother Earth's Obituary

A blanket of grime, suffocating shroud,
smog thickened, a poisonous cloud.
Cities wear a grey tuxedo,
born from Industry's might.
A sacrifice willingly made to,
'God of Progress'.
A gloomy sight.

Our atmosphere, a toxic veil.
Our waters, a chocolate-brown trail.
Our forests, a receding hairline.
'Save this planet before it's too late',
A daily headline.

"We must do better,"
declares a concerned citizen,
rolling down the windows,
of his latest diesel gulping machine.

"Let's plant more trees & save this planet,"
says, the CEO of a coffee chain.
While travelling to his office
in his private corporate plane.

"Keep the forests clean"
tweets an earnest teen,
while trashing his can in the valley
he was last seen.

Muffled words, empty promises,
a hollow show.
Half-brewed ideas,
actions slow.
Our planet is losing the fight.
Hypocrisy triumphs, a disgraceful plight.

– unscribbled_verses

# An Outcast

Take me away
Take me far away from these thoughts.
Like a bright red apple,
rotting from within its core,
trying to blend in with the ones in the basket.
I don't belong in this basket,
and nor do I wish to.
Do people remember that apple?
Or was it just such a waste?
Oh, how can one find such peace in silence,
in one's own suffering?
Ridiculous it has been so far.
I'm starting to find humor in the mirror,
and the stars have never seemed prettier.
Oh, what are these chains even made of?
Like rainfall in a drought-stricken land
why does my knife seem so red?
The blade shows me my eyes.
If only it could see my heart for once.
The world would be peaceful again.

– Ivnat

# A Winter Night

Can you hear it—the silence?
That lasts for a moment or two.
Let it caress your heart.
Listen to the rhythms that speak back to you.

Slip back into sweet oblivion,
throwing away the new found epiphany—
That the world might start spinning again.
If it must, then let it be.

You will be back soon enough,
behind the window that you were before.
But if I promise you eternity,
will you stay just a second more?

– Anisha

# Resilience

*Through pain, loss, scars, and the will
to rise again*

# An Ode To A City Flower

Have you ever seen a flower grow
in a city where humans perish?
The men, the women, the dreamers,
all perish,
before they get to cherish,
the dreams they worked to build.

A flower grows in cracks of unscreaming dreams,
in houses where voices die,
where babies are silent and their mothers cry.
Generations of pain, all seeping into the wall,
the flower grows; accepts it all.

And when you have consumed such pain,
even when sun eats your youth away,
even when rain comes only once a day,
even when unkind kids stomp their feet,
you live on.

Such a futile life, my dear flower you live,
so much life in you,
for a life that lasts a week!
and yet, in it, beauty and meaning I seek.

For is it not strength,
to stand with tendril roots,
grasp on unkind walls
and grow to be less weak?

– Jay Vira

# Point Nemo

Past nights lead to brighter days,
a quiet listener, with less to say.
No longer do I sleep with dry tears.
It's the hollow self that I now fear.

I read about Point Nemo and its distant shore.
Life's getting warm, I see much more.
A safer place from the rich's spoils.
A place of rest far from the daily soil.

When overworked and deeply strained,
crash on me, for this day I've trained.
Far from home, yet near to the flower,
I'll wait for you through every decaying hour.

Thus, nights seem brighter than the day,
Though from Point Nemo, I only gaze away.
Oh, burning satellites, if rest you seek,
Point Nemo's nest is yours to keep.

Thoughts begin to change and heart sways.
What comes to Point Nemo, in its arms it stays.

– Priyanshu Pratap

# Growing Up in the Shadow

I grew up in the shadow of others' fame,
a younger sibling, always in the game.
Their achievements loomed, a constant stress,
I felt like a ghost, invisible, I guess.

I tried to find my voice, but it was drowned,
by the noise of their success, a constant sound.
I felt lost and alone, like a fading light,
a small, insignificant star, in a vast, dark night.

I'm still searching for my place, my own identity,
a sense of belonging, a sense of being free.
But the shadow of their greatness still looms near,
a constant reminder of my own doubts and fears.

– Sakshi Kulkarni

# Kaudi – The Blanket

In her last years, Nani spent
all her time stitching Kaudi.
She did tens of them and gave
them away to her loved ones.

She would gather all the
old clothes, cut them up,
stitch them in patches on
stretch of old sarees.

These blankets she stitched
so meticulously, almost
every hour of every day,
looked like her biography.

All the childhood memories,
scattered in the red patches.
Her teenage days in the
checkered yellow ones..

In the glittery embroidery
on the borders.

Maybe about her first love
or a crush if there was one.

I got the last one of
her final work.

One of the nights,
the green patches in mine,
told me all about the raw guavas
in her father's backyard.

Now that I keep thinking
about those violet, brown
and the pink patches that
haven't yet talked.

Maybe that's where the rest
of the world's libraries hide.

– unsung_seagull

# Of Spring and Rain

It's a centuries old tale,
long forgotten yet felt,
of a girl with flowers for hair
and a boy who loved to play.

Every year when spring came,
she would dance in golly grace,
while he sat near his window,
for hours he stayed.

As time passed by,
fall came along,
with it falling down
all of the girl's jolly songs.

She would weep and weep
while her hair fell out,
wishing that spring would come around.
For love is brutal as they say,
he would always tell her,
"You're still the same."

Her sadness now his own,
as he held her close,
tears fell to the ground,
and with it she flourished once again
because she was the
spring and he was her rain.

– Tamanna Bhargava

# Welcome To My Happy Place!

My key to happiness is found when I enter home to look for him and call his name.

After a warm hug and conversation on the sofa, we admire the sunset

that shows our happy faces in the glass of the window frame.

Through the narrow gap of the window, enters the sunlight,

he illuminates my path of life, and that's all I need to shine bright.

The wind chime is swaying to the wind on the balcony and making clinks,

like I get carried away looking into his eyes, which can soothe my emotions with his single blink.

Just like the handprints on the wall and the footprints on the tile,

he makes my cheeks blush pink and red filled with love painted with his happy smiles.

My home has a heart that is his, and that's where I stay, wherever his love is, I always find my way.

– Gayathri

# Rose Upon Failure

Rise, Dear. Rise.
Rise upon your failure.
It's ok to not be constantly right.
Winners aren't always successful overnight.

They cursed me under their breath,
buried my dreams in the name of culture.
They crushed me to the earth,
thinking that I would fear their torture.
But I rose.
I rose upon my failure with an oath
that I would form my brighter future.
Either sooner or later, but for sure.

As my eyelids got heavier, I opened them wider with the
help of flares.
The flares of passion that lit my brain.

With the assurance that success would come to me,
I made my dreams real, turning their words into myth.

Sleepless nights, there weren't just one or two,
but all of them don't bother me now!
All I want to say to myself is 'Thank you',
for resolving to take a vow,

The vow to rise upon failure!

– Parmitha

# I Kissed Another Man

For the longest time
I have worn my heart on my sleeve
he promised me forever,
and buried it
right under the ground,
where we built our home.
It's in the past.
I kissed another man,
and we're even now.

My heart now guards
the cemetery I made
for the lovers who betrayed me.

I roll their promises
and smoke 'em with my coffee
but once in a while, I visit
the graveyard
to check if anyone left
a new flower
for my lonely heart.

– Kanika Suri

# Flowers Underneath the Sea

Rivers of thoughts pour
into the sea of my mind each day.
Some create waves and
some ebb away.
But most drown and
go to the gardens I create
that only I can visit
when I close my eyes
and spend time in their presence.

I watch as hope blooms
and courage blossoms
in this state of deep contemplation.
As I take some moments of self-reflection,
I notice the change they make in my perceptions to deal
with the same situation.

How I wish I could show you
the world through my eyes,
but till the time you are ready
to listen to me,
I'll keep writing the stories

of these flowers underneath the sea
with the hope that you will find the will
and learn to swim in this sea someday.

– Shaymi Shah

# Architecture of Loneliness

While your sibling was breaking toys,
your mother was giving you lessons
on building blocks of life.
You grew up as an elder child,
tossing your feelings
like tissue papers,
using jaggery as
a replacement ingredient
when you run out of sugar,
applying balm on the back of
your exhausted mother and shushing
the galaxy sprouting out of
your mind's mesmerizing museum.

Suddenly,
you're seventeen—an option for emergencies,
eighteen—your grandmother's
unhinged pastime,
nineteen—an old invitation card
ready to be discarded
into the dustbin.
Self-doubt is hammered into

the wall of your forehead.
Your eyes reek of misery.
You carry a body smudged with
centuries of grief.

Soon,
you'll be twenty-something,
leaving your fragrance everywhere
like a flower kneaded into a human.
Butterflies will look up to you.
If someone asks about your transition,
you will say, I discovered a poem,
which took me to a hut of self-love
for which I abandoned
my grand architecture of loneliness.

– Khatija Khan

# Om Namah Shivay!

As my eyes turn a little towards the sky,

my heart flutters as I see you watching me at this site.

The letters that I've wrote to you,

the prayers that I've cried,

You have blessed me with love

What more can I ask for tonight?

My soul was oblivious that I found you in every particle
of life

when I was searching for you in lost paths of time.

I haven't read all your scriptures,

neither do I know every mantra you like,

But still you were beside me all this time.

So how can I forget to pray to you tonight?

Every piece of me is incomplete without chanting

Om namah shivay!

Om namah shivay!

– Ridd

# The Sun That Never Rose Again

She freely heaved a sigh of relief,
as the dark and dusky night set in.
Serenely, she gazed out of the window,
realizing the moon was nowhere seen.

All the miseries that bothered inside,
all the judgements that burdened her,
felt like far away shrinking clouds,
resembling momentary winds of thunder.

An unexpected solace and calmness,
harmonizing breath of satisfaction.
A hallucination or the inevitable destiny?
She no longer solicited an answer to her question.

As she drifted through the negativities,
her soul re-discovered priceless peace;
With an unregretful smile of comfort,
she pacified the chaotic tides with ease.

She was the wick that endured the flame,
she was the panacea for her pain,
she was the moon that needed a break,
she was the sun that never rose again!

– Deepti G Shastry

# Broken Soul

Flickering lights, the room turns gray,
headphones on to drown the day.
Scrolling through ghosts on a cracked-up screen,
hiding in pixels, stuck in between.

Tears fall slow, they don't hit the ground,
caught in a loop where pain's profound.
Heart on autoplay, same sad song,
lyrics of loss, it plays too long.

I text but delete, no words feel right,
conversations fade into the night.
Reflections stare with empty eyes,
a fragile mask, a thin disguise.

But in the chaos, there's still a beat,
a glitch in the dark, a hope discreet.
Maybe one day, I'll take control,
and reboot this broken soul.

– Abhishek H Rathod

# The Sea and I

The wind howls in different tones,
an ode to voices long unheard.
Waves claw at shattered walls,
windows gaping like wounds.
Polaroids hang heavy
on damp ceilings,
salt creeping through edges,
as if the sea, too, mourns.

On the shore,
a widow hums a lullaby,
lulling the coast to dreams,
hands search for husband's voice
in shells unbroken.
Plastic soldiers drown in dunes,
forgotten battles against time.
A fish seller casts debts,
sinner's eyes soften to a saint's
as if the sea could return
what it once took.

An old man curses fate,
scribbling forgotten letters

his daughter taught,
with trembling feet,
but tide, a thief,
ran away with them.

A lighthouse flickers,
narrating tales to passing ships—
"I'm not cracked by yearning."

But as dusk descends,
the waves retreat,
horizon blushes with possibility.
Among the wreckage,
a child builds tomorrow
hurling worries
at the arms of the sea.

– Mrittika Chatterjee

# Killer

I killed the boy,
who smiled merrily
and held his father's hand
In deep trust.

The boy,
whose mother's kisses',
moist imprint, embraced
his chubby cheeks.

The boy,
whose shoe laces
were untied.
And yet,
he kicked the ball merrily.

I butchered that boy,
strangled his throat,
stabbed his guts.

And while his blood
gushed out,
flooding the floor;

I became but
a coffin,
carrying him around!

– Rwitabrata Chatterjee

# A Dandelion

I saw a little dandelion floating in the water,
not knowing its journey.
I looked for a while at her,
pondered how she would bloom if I put her in a pot.
I picked her up half-drenched on my finger,
as delicate as a baby she cried for help.
So, I sowed her in a pot to see her flower.
Seasons passed but I never saw her blossom.
I put her in the wrong place, oh Nature!
Not every soil can harbour every plant.

– Aakriti Singh

# Braveheart

My nonage tales were marked,
With quite a few gruesome episodes of self-apocalypse.
I used to often take offense then if I did not win,
used to recoil within my cocooned self to nurse my injured pride.
And after each defeat, I would declare in pain,
"It is an unfair life and a totally unfair game!"

But then I realized eventually that,
it did not mean the end of the world.
For even after those agonizing defeats,
my hopes and dreams would remain intact.
And each defeat chiselled a little better version of me,
channelizing my painfully gathered experience and wisdom towards winning the world.
This new me could see intrepid dreams.
This new me had finally learned to fall with grace and pride.
For by then, I had learned to never be defeated in spirit,
while diving deep to face the trials and tribulations of life.

– Indrani Chowdhury

# Eternal Night

I bleed in expensive wine.
White walls wear jewellery of bone,
poked, sliced and dined, a canvas so fine.
Store my heart in the treasury, alone.

The world bleeds monotone, a dull, muted ache,
a symphony of grey where colors forgot their song.
I crave a final verse, a vibrant mistake,
a masterpiece etched in blood, where I truly belong.

The city sleeps, a carcass beneath a smog-choked sky,
streetlights cast macabre grins, where hope goes to die.
I yearn for a terror that rips the night's veil in two,
a crimson spillage that paints the dawn a grotesque hue.

Tonight, a canvas trembles, a masterpiece to ignite,
a concerto of screams in a final, desperate fight.
Let the final brushstroke be agony, raw and bright,
for in this macabre dance, I become the eternal night.

– Jatin Targaryen

# Knocked Down, But Not Out

This year came swinging, and I felt every hit,
dreams undone, plans torn bit by bit.
It shook the ground beneath my feet,
turned every triumph into retreat.

But I've learned a thing or two from the fight,
how to stand my ground, how to hold on tight.
Adversity's a teacher, harsh and unkind,
but it chisels the edges, sharpens the mind.

This wasn't my year, and that's okay.
The storms it brought won't always stay.
I've patched the cracks, rebuilt the walls,
learned to rise faster after the falls.

Next year, might still throw its punches too,
but I've got scars now, proof I came through.
Resilience isn't pretty, but it's fierce and true—
I'm walking forward, no matter the view.

So here's to tomorrow, to what's yet to appear.
This year knocked me down,
but it didn't end here.

– Chhavi Lamba

# Her Lingering Shadows

Blood drained from her brittle bones,
moonlight veils her cinnamon skin.
Eyes that once held a million dreams
now stare lifeless—forsaken, a diabolical sin.

Perhaps she lived a borrowed life,
and as the grim reaper knocked her door,
the debt she repaid and left behind,
secrets entombed deep in her grave.

Like a madman, I pace through the night,
clutching old receipts, chasing fading signs—
Signs. So many signs.
Memories that dwindle, refusing to die.

Her voice lingers in the winds that howl
through empty streets that mock my fall.
I sift through ashes where her laughter burns.
Silent nights witness my yearns.

Crushed lilies decay on her doorstep.
I knock, though the sound will never reach her ear.
Dead sunflowers don't bloom the next morning,
yet I wait, hoping they might.

– Rajvi Gupta

# Stitching Hearts

A gloomy summer afternoon,
the sky is dark enough
to roar and say,
"It's going to rain soon."
And the people around chanting,
from time to time,
"It's raining heavily these days."
And you sit there silently,
trying to absorb everything.
The mild breeze whispers to you,
"Hey, I am here with you."
And you smile unknowingly,
when the breeze kisses your messy hair.

Your heart has always been,
like those fresh clay pots.
So easy to break again.
And you sit there,
listening to the silence,
and trying to throw away
all the heartbreaks
in the vast river.

Can the Ganges hold your pain?
You believe it can.
And it will.
You will stitch your broken heart this time.
Alone,
with no fancy threads or perfect embroidery set.
With the Ganges flowing by and divinity sinking in,
you will stitch your heart.

– Aliva Dutta

# The Girl At The Ocean

I see a girl at the edge of the ocean,
her toes just dangling by.
She stares at the water,
like a forsaken lover,
but she never steps inside.

"Don't be afraid.
I'll hold your hand all the way,"
The water sings its song.
She stares at her hand,
traces patterns on the sand,
never listens to its calls.

And she watches as the others go by,
holding onto the ocean tide,
she smiles to herself.
Oh what wonderful hell
to be stuck on this side of life,
but dear ocean, you were never mine to ride.

I think I'm in love with the girl at the ocean,
Her toes just dangling by.
I'll wait by the water,
like a forsaken lover,
hoping one day she'll step inside.


– Praneeta

# Woman

I grew up, a girl becoming a woman,
carrying questions I never asked for.
Why did I, in my innocence,
face shadows of abuse so dark?

Was it my fault,
the cruel laughter of society?
Or a silent God watching from above?

My questions remain unanswered,
yet, here I stand—
A woman who carries her fears,
her scars hidden behind gentle smiles.

But I am not just me.
I am every girl, every woman.
What I felt, what I faced,
so many others have too.

I am not the only one,
yet I am not just another one.
In this world, among shadows, I find light,
in the kindness of men who protect,
who stand as walls, not chains.

This is the world I live in.
You live in.
We all live in.
A world where angels and evils
wear the same face.

– Riya

# Golden Heart

Sometimes, I ponder if my heart is pure,
but each time I seek, the truth feels unsure.
Not a heart of gold, but one that brightly glows,
a heart that feels deeply, as everyone knows.

It sparkles and shines, yet it trembles with fear,
crying softly when loved ones aren't near.
It beats with a rhythm that echoes my soul,
a heart that can fracture, yet still seeks to be whole.

When you leave, my heart aches, it knows the pain,
scared of the moments when love feels like rain.
Though not forged from gold, it's rich in its way,
a heart full of passion, come night or come day.

So here I stand, with this heart that I hold,
a glowing reminder that love is not sold.
It may not be perfect, but it's honest and bright,
a heart that shines fiercely, a beacon of light.

– Vidhi Goel

# I'm a Mother

I'm a mother…
I tremble and stumble,
piled high with whining chores.
I mumble and grumble,
with no retirement in sight—time's woes.

I'm a 24-hour cook, nanny,
chauffeur, tutor, mentor…
Endless roles, I must say!
I'm an auditor, advisor, counselor, and analyst,
unpaid, counting the many roles I play.

Mandatory tantrums and taunts,
fired at me in dismay.
I become a sponge,
soaking it all throughout the day.

My mother's house in my mind
with closed eyes, I stay.
I once lived like a bird,
counting each passing day.

Chin up! Make-up!
I'm a proud mother, I say!
I need not be a model,
to ramp walk and slay.

I'm a mother, I'm a warrior,
I must say,
from the day I conceived,
till my last day.

– Ayesha Naaz

# A Fabric For the Soul

I have threads of memories,
braided together,
with moments good and bad,
emotions happy and sad,
moving together endlessly connecting.

I have threads of memories,
braided together.
Would you care to look?
Would you dare to understand?
A blizzard at the shore of a golden desert,
Yes, it's an absurd sight.

I have threads of memories,
braided together.
The old knit well with each other,
the new seem just as fine.
There are a few I wished to leave,
but this greed of mine to hold on to things,
Scarred my fingers as my stubborn soul
fixed them together.

I have threads of memories,
braided together.
A few I have qualms about,
yet, some too perfect to be missed.
They broke me and built me up again.
It's not just a body but the soul that evolves,
following this path of reminiscence,
standing at the culmination,
as the threads dance and join together.

– Chhaaya Pant

# A Mother's Dream

I dared to dream as a woman, and I heard my mother say,
"We can never make a choice, only follow the societal
script."
And I said…
A woman's pain is her voice unheard.
A mother's dreams crash at the feet of your success.
The stories of her sacrifices,
perhaps, you will never see on a library's bookshelves,
but they are still worth sharing.

A daughter's pain is replacing her mother's arms
with her own when she wants to cry.
But dreams, they do not wait.
"Yes mother, I am doing alright here," she will say,
"But not without you," are words
that will never escape her lips.
Oh world, listen to me.
Dreams, they do not wait.
I will cry, I can scream, I could be scared,
but I shall not falter.
For a mother's dream is saving her daughter,
but a daughter's dream is saving her mother.

– Anashwara R

# Almighty, My Hope and Abode

Living on the edges of survival,
living to die or maybe dying each day to live,
being distorted yet attempting to thrive,
being mindless yet attempting to enlighten,
reality that is vaguer than fiction
factions which are more desperate than imagination.

Then when reality was but a few leaves and twigs,
and friendships were the cause of existence to eternity,
then when food was a distraction from newfound discoveries in sport
and trust needed just a moment of play,
then when energy rebounded at every command from the dusty ground,
there, let my sunshine be.

Let not the sickness of the destitute force, distort the very moment that I long.
Let not anger and strife find my utopia in the divide.

Let this be my goal and my prayer,
to hope for humanity from my Almighty.
For at least there be peace where my abode is to be.

– Roy Jennita Sundari I

# Black Dupatta

It was so soon.
The black dupatta
covered my head yet again.
It seemed like only yesterday
that I had it during mourning.

I heard the news again.
We had lost another soul,
who lived amongst us
with aspirations, dreams,
whose age was merely 50.

So, today, I wear the dupatta,
tears roll down my cheeks,
wondering why God does this,
taking soul after soul,
life after life,
with hopes, dreams unfulfilled.

The journey, uncertain,
The length, unpredictable,
The road-risky,
Why?

We never know for sure,
What will happen next?

All I wish for
God can spare me,
the use of the black dupatta,
ever so often.

– Harmeet Dhillon